BACTERIA

BACTERIA

HOWARD AND MARGERY FACKLAM

TWENTY-FIRST CENTURY BOOKS
A DIVISION OF HENRY HOLT AND COMPANY
NEW YORK

Twenty-First Century Books
A Division of Henry Holt and Company, Inc.
115 West 18th Street
New York, NY 10011

Henry Holt ® and colophon are trademarks of
Henry Holt and Company, Inc.
Publishers since 1866

Published in Canada by Fitzhenry & Whiteside Ltd.
195 Allstate Parkway, Markham, Ontario L3R 4T8

Library of Congress Cataloging-in-Publication Data
Facklam, Howard.
    Bacteria / Howard and Margery Facklam. — 1st ed.
      p. cm. — (Invaders)
    1. Microbiology—Juvenile literature. [1. Bacteria. 2. Microbiology.]
    I. Facklam, Margery. II. Title. III. Series.
    QR57.F33 1994
    589.9—dc20   94–25430
                                                              CIP
                                                              AC

ISBN 0-8050-2857-9
First Edition 1994

Printed in the United States of America
All first editions are printed on acid-free paper ∞.

10 9 8 7 6 5 4 3 2 1

Photo Credits
Cover: David Scharf/Peter Arnold, Inc.; p. 9 (tl): David Scharf/Peter Arnold, Inc.; p. 9 (tr): David M. Phillips/Visuals Unlimited; p. 9 (b): Omikron/Science Source/Photo Researchers, Inc.; pp. 11, 14: CNRI/SPL/Science Source/Photo Researchers, Inc.; pp. 16, 27, 29: courtesy of the National Library of Medicine; p. 16 (inset): Dr. J. Burgess/SPL/Science Source/Photo Researchers, Inc.; p. 17: Jean-Loup Charmet/Science Source/Photo Researchers, Inc.; p. 19: Michael Gabridge/Visuals Unlimited; pp. 23, 29 (inset), 48: The Bettmann Archive; p. 25: D. Phillips/Science Source/Photo Researchers, Inc.; p. 34: reprinted with permission, from *Biology: Life on Earth*, 3d. ed. by Audesirk and Audesirk, © 1993 Macmillan College Publishing; p. 35: A. E. Zuckerman/Liaison International; p. 37 (l): Fletcher and Bayliss/Photo Researchers, Inc.; p. 37 (r), 55: courtesy of the U.S. Department of Agriculture; p. 39: Leonard Lessin/Peter Arnold, Inc.; pp. 43 (all), 46: Charles Orear/Westlight; p. 51: K. G. Murti/Visuals Unlimited; p. 52: Matt Meadows/Peter Arnold, Inc.; p. 54: R. L. Brinster/Peter Arnold, Inc.

CONTENTS

1

BACTERIA EVERYWHERE

Not all extra body weight is caused by eating too much. Each of us carries about a quarter pound (112 grams) that can be blamed on bacteria. We are literally teeming with bacteria. They live in deep crevices of our teeth, all over our skin, in our hair, and under our fingernails. Billions of bacteria live in our intestines, where they make essential vitamins and protect us from diseases. We eat and breathe bacteria all the time.

Bacteria are microbes, tiny organisms that can be seen only with the aid of a microscope. But nature is unpredictable, and recently scientists discovered a kind of bacteria that can be seen with the naked eye. They live inside a tropical fish, and they are millions of times larger than the average bacteria. One researcher said that comparing these bacteria to other bacteria is like comparing battleships to canoes.

Scientists believe that bacteria have been on earth for about three and a half million years, and during that time they have adapted to all kinds of environments. They are found in Arctic snow, in boiling hot springs, and 6 miles (nearly 10 kilometers) down on the ocean floor. While drilling for oil, scientists found bacteria in rock cores 1,300 feet (390 meters) deep in the earth, and NASA teams found them 19 miles (30 kilometers) out in space. A teaspoon of good farm soil contains about 10 million bacteria, and one acre (0.4 hectare) of this bacteria-rich soil houses 200 to 500 pounds (91 to 227 kilograms) of microbes. It has been estimated that microbes make up 5 to 25 times the total mass of all other animal life combined. This means there is more unseen life on earth than life that can be seen.

Microbes have a bad reputation for causing diseases, but that is far from their only function. They are also nature's recyclers. Everything that dies is broken down by bacteria and other microbes into simple materials that can be used for new life. Without these natural recyclers, carbon, nitrogen, and other elements necessary for life would be unavailable to new plants and animals, and life on earth would soon cease to exist.

Even though they are primitive one-celled organisms, bacteria perform the same life functions as all more highly developed organisms. They use energy, grow, make wastes, and reproduce. A bacterial cell is surrounded by a membrane that holds the contents of the cell together and acts as a gatekeeper, controlling what goes in and out of the cell. Most bacteria also have a wall around the outside of the membrane. This wall, which may be flexible or rigid, gives the cell its shape. The wall also affects the bacteria's susceptibility to antibiotics and protective secretions such as tears and saliva. Some bacteria also have a sticky coating called a capsule over the cell walls, which gives extra protection and helps individual cells stick together.

Bacteria come in three basic shapes: cocci, which are round; bacilli, which are rods; and spirilla, which are spirals. When two bacteria stick together to form a pair, they are called *diplo*. One kind of diplococcus (two rounded bacteria stuck together) causes pneumonia. When several bacteria stick together and form a chain, they are called *strepto*. A severe throat infection known as strep throat is caused by a type of streptococcus. When bacteria stick together to form clumps or clusters, they are called *staphylo*. Boils and some serious infections such as meningitis are caused by *Staphylococcus* bacteria. Bacilli, the rod-shaped bacteria, are usually separate, but some do stick together end to end. They form long, funguslike filaments that were once thought to be a fungus rather than a bacterium. One type of these bacilli, mycobacterium, causes tuberculosis in humans.

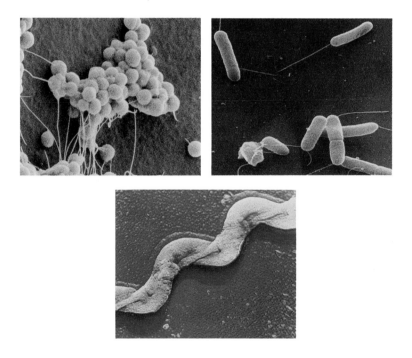

The three basic shapes of bacteria. The cocci are the normally harmless Staphylococcus *bacteria that live in and on our bodies. The bacilli with flagella are* Escherichia coli, *which live in our intestines. The spirillum, or spirochete, is* Leptospira, *which lives in mammals, especially domestic animals.*

Some kinds of bacteria don't move at all. Others have tiny hairlike structures called flagella that beat in a circular motion. Flagella may be at one end of a bacterium or all around the cell. They beat so fast they look like a blur under a microscope. In fact, the flagella of one type of bacteria were clocked at 2,400 beats per minute. Some spiral-shaped bacteria move with a corkscrew motion. Other kinds glide or creep along on a slimy mucus secretion that oozes out ahead of them.

Even though bacteria have no brains or nervous systems, they respond to changes in their environment. Bacteria can sense the presence of food and move toward it. They can also sense and move away from at least 20 different toxic, or injurious, chemicals. Recently, when researchers were studying *E. coli (Escherichia coli)*, the bacteria that live in our intestines, they discovered "nose spots," which turned out to be specific structures that can detect chemicals. There is also evidence that even without a brain, bacteria have primitive memories. They can remember for as long as 60 seconds, which is a long time in the life of bacteria. Other bacteria have been found to contain a chain of tiny cube-shaped magnets made of the mineral magnetite. In the Northern Hemisphere, these bacteria line themselves up toward the magnetic north, while bacteria in the Southern Hemisphere line themselves up toward the magnetic south.

When scientists talk about bacterial growth, they don't just mean that one cell grows bigger. They are talking about reproduction, or cell multiplication. Most bacteria multiply by dividing. One cell divides into two cells, and each of the two new cells is exactly like the first, or mother, cell. Each is half the size, but they grow. Most bacteria divide every two or three hours, but some divide every 15 minutes and others may wait as long as 16 hours. If just one bacterium divided every 20 minutes and didn't run out of food or poison itself

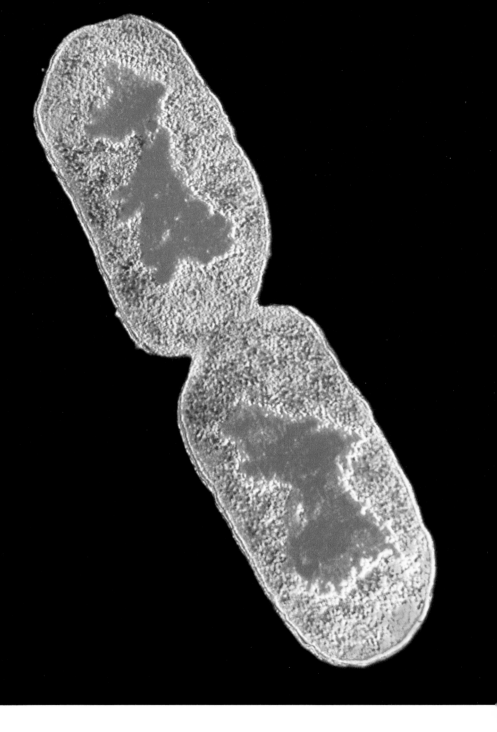

A bacterial cell dividing. The process produces two identical versions of the original cell.

with its own accumulated wastes, in 24 hours it would become a colony of bacteria weighing two million pounds (907,985 kilograms). And all the bacteria in that two-million-pound colony would be exactly like the single original cell that first divided.

This type of simple asexual reproduction, called binary fission, does not produce individuals with any differences. The new cells are clones. DNA, which stands for deoxyribonucleic acid, contains the complete genetic information of a cell in the form of a code. After reproduction, the DNA in each new bacterium is exactly the same as the DNA in the original mother cell. The genetic information in the cloned bacterium DNA has not mixed with DNA from any other cells.

Some kinds of bacteria do have a simple kind of sexual process, called conjugation, in which two bacterial cells temporarily join and exchange parts of their DNA. The advantage of conjugation is variety. By mixing their DNA, each cell has a chance to become different in some way.

When a population of bacteria is growing fast and using up its food supply, many of them dehydrate and produce thick, tough spore coats. As spores, the bacteria can rest and survive the bad times. Spores can stay alive for hundreds, even thousands, of years. In the ruins of ancient Rome, live bacterial spores have been found that were buried more than 1,900 years ago. Spores 5,800 years old have been taken out of sediment on the floor of the Pacific Ocean, off the coast of Southern California. But the record for the oldest living spores goes to those found in sediments dredged from Elk Lake in Minnesota. They were between 7,000 and 7,500 years old.

When spores find a favorable environment that provides warmth, moisture, and food, they can become active again. They absorb water, break down their spore coats, and form new cell walls. Some spores, however, can resist very high temperatures, and their bacteria can be deadly. Botulin, the most powerful poison in the world, causes botulism. The toxin is produced by bacteria that can survive as spores in boiling water for up to five hours. This toxin affects the human nervous system, and even the tiniest amount is often fatal. Foods canned in home kitchens are most often the ones that contain botulin toxin because the foods aren't heated long enough at temperatures high enough to kill the bacteria. The canned foods bought in stores are safe because they are superheated with steam. But just to be on the safe side, always throw away cans of food that are dented or rusty or have a bulge because they might contain dangerous bacterial toxins.

Spores of bacteria that cause gangrene and tetanus are common in soil and on dirty objects outdoors. Most living things are aerobic, which means they must have oxygen to survive. The bacteria that cause tetanus and gangrene, however, are anaerobic, which means they do not use oxygen. In fact, they cannot survive when oxygen is present. In deep wounds, where they are away from the air, the spores of these bacteria become active and multiply fast, causing severe infections that eat away tissue and can cause death. Wounds like these can be treated by opening them and flooding them with oxygen, which kills the bacteria. During the Civil War, the most common reason for amputations was gangrene that raged in the wounds of soldiers left lying on battlefields or in unsanitary tent hospitals. Today, if a person steps on a rusty nail or has some other deep injury that is not easy to clean out, a tetanus shot prevents these dangerous bacteria from taking over.

Like all cells, bacteria have sudden, unexplained changes in their genes called mutations. With a life that lasts from only minutes to a few hours, new generations of bacteria appear quickly, and a mutation can spread through a

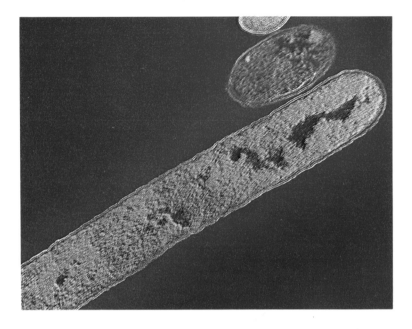

The bacterium that causes tetanus. This bacillus lives in soil and as a parasite in animals such as cattle.

whole population of bacteria like lightning. Through their billions of years on earth, mutations have allowed bacteria to adapt to all kinds of changes in the environment. This great variety has made bacteria some of the most numerous and successful organisms on earth.

2
WHO
FOUND
BACTERIA?

Every living thing is made of cells, and everything a living thing does is done by the cells that make it up. No one had ever heard of a cell until a 29-year-old Englishman, Robert Hooke, coined the word in 1665 after looking at a thin slice of cork under a microscope he had made. Hooke thought that each microscopic section of cork looked like the tiny cubicles, or cells, where monks lived in monasteries.

At about the same time in the Netherlands, Antonie van Leeuwenhoek was also making a microscope, although he had never heard of Hooke, his microscope, or cells. Van Leeuwenhoek worked in a fabric shop, where he examined threads for flaws with a magnifying glass. But he was also an amateur scientist, and he was fascinated by lenses. Hooke's microscope had two rather crude lenses, but van Leeuwenhoek's single-lens instrument, which magnified objects up to 200 times their size, was so beautifully crafted that lens experts today still aren't sure exactly how he made it. And with his microscope, van Leeuwenhoek saw into a world that changed science forever.

One of the first things van Leeuwenhoek looked at was a drop of water, where he saw all kinds of "wretched beasties" squirming around. When he scraped a bit of "white matter" from his teeth, he saw "tiny animalcules" in this material. Van Leeuwenhoek could not have known he was the first person to see bacteria. Nor could he have known that another 200 years would go by before tiny creatures like those he saw were proven to be one of the microbes that cause infectious diseases.

For as far back as such events were recorded, we know that great epidemics raged through towns and cities. In 430 B.C., a plague that attacked people with raging fever, intense thirst, bloody tongue, and skin blisters killed half the

Antonie van Leeuwenhoek demonstrating his microscopes to Catherine of England.
Inset: Van Leeuwenhoek's drawings of the "animalcules" (bacteria) from the human mouth he saw with his microscopes.

people in Athens, Greece. In A.D. 166, Roman soldiers returned from battle in Syria with a plague so terrible that every morning wagons loaded with bodies were taken from Rome to be buried in the countryside. This was an attack of bubonic plague, and it ravished Europe for 15 years, killing one-fourth of the population.

Leprosy, tuberculosis, cholera, and diphtheria were common diseases, and nobody knew what caused them. In their ignorance, people believed that diseases were the work of evil spirits and demons. Often the victim was blamed, as though the disease was a punishment from the gods or the curse of an enemy.

If diseases could come from the spirit world, it is not hard to understand why people also believed that life could spring from nonliving materials. For more than 2,000 years, this belief, called spontaneous generation, was accepted as fact. Anyone could see that flies emerged from rotting flesh, which made it easy to believe that rotting meat gave birth to flies. Toward the end of the 1500s, the physician Jan Baptista van Helmont wrote, "The emanations arising from the bottom of marshes bring forth frogs, snails, leeches, herbs, and a good many other things."

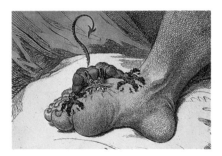

In the long search to find the causes of diseases, one of the most amazing leaps was the enormous one Edward Jenner took in 1798. He found a way to prevent a disease without know-

A cartoon illustrating the belief that diseases are caused by demons. The person is suffering from gout, which is actually caused by a buildup of uric acid in the joints.

ing what caused the disease or why the prevention worked. Smallpox was a fearsome disease that people had dreaded for centuries. If it didn't kill a person, it left the victim's face scarred with pits. Cowpox was a similar but milder disease, and Jenner noticed that people who caught cowpox did not get smallpox. Although Jenner was successful in using fluid from cowpox sores to vaccinate people against smallpox, another 150 years would pass before scientists knew that a virus caused smallpox and what the virus actually looked like.

No one had heard of a germ theory of disease until the 1860s, when Louis Pasteur and Robert Koch came up with convincing evidence that infectious diseases were caused by tiny microorganisms and not by evil spirits. Pasteur, a French chemist and microbiologist, was consulted by people in the French silk industry to find out why the silkworms were dying. He isolated and identified two different bacteria that were causing diseases in the worms. Pasteur then recommended that all the diseased worms be destroyed and that the industry start fresh with new, healthy worms. Pasteur's advice helped save this major French industry.

Pasteur made many other discoveries. He found that microorganisms cause foods to spoil and decompose. Before this discovery, chemists thought the spoilage and decomposition of foods were just natural chemical changes at work. Pasteur also found the organisms that cause milk to turn sour, and he developed a method to destroy those organisms. This method is known today as pasteurization. In 1864, Pasteur finally laid to rest the theory of spontaneous generation when he proved that all life must come from life, and that even microorganisms reproduce.

Science sometimes moves forward in surprising steps that may seem small, but that turn out to make big leaps possible. One such small step was 17-year-old William Perkin's discovery of aniline dyes made from coal tar. The big leap occurred when Robert Koch, a German scientist, found that bacteria absorbed the aniline dyes, making them easy to identify under a microscope. Before Koch's discovery, biologists had been staining bacteria with vegetable dyes, but they were not well absorbed and made identification difficult.

Koch also developed the rules for growing bacterial cultures that are still followed today. He discovered a way to grow mixed groups of bacteria and then separate them into pure cultures. The usual practice in laboratories at the time was to raise bacteria in blood serum or meat broth. But in those mediums it was impossible to separate the different kinds of bacteria. Koch began to grow his bacteria on agar, a gelatinlike substance made from seaweed. He also added broth to make a richer food for the bacteria. One of Koch's assistants, Julius Petri, made a shallow, covered glass dish to

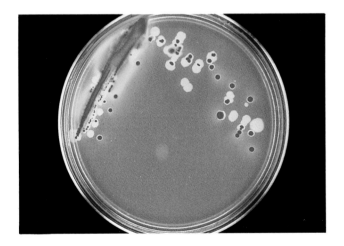

A petri dish with colonies of two different kinds of bacteria growing on agar. Scientists grow bacteria in this way to study the color, shape, and speed of growth of colonies, and to see how different bacteria interact with one another.

hold the agar, and it worked so well that since then his dishes, now called petri dishes, have been used in laboratories around the world.

The first step in starting a new culture of bacteria is making sure no other organisms contaminate or mix with it. A thin piece of wire with a small loop at the end is heated to kill any bacteria on it. The sterile loop is then used to streak the surface of clean agar with whatever infected tissue is to be studied. The petri dish is covered and put into an incubator, which is kept at human body temperature (98.6°F [37°C]) for one to two days. During this time, the different kinds of bacteria present in the tissue grow into separate clumps or colonies on the agar. The colony of each kind of bacteria has its own distinctive shape and color, which makes it easy to identify. A loopful of a specific kind of bacteria can then be transferred to another petri dish and allowed to grow. This method made it possible for the first time to isolate bacteria and identify the ones causing specific diseases.

In 1876, Koch identified and isolated the bacterium that causes anthrax, a widespread and fatal disease in sheep and cattle. In 1882, he identified the tuberculosis bacterium, and a year later the cholera bacterium. By the beginning of the 1900s, researchers using Koch's rules, staining techniques, and agar cultures had identified most of the bacteria harmful to humans.

A severe epidemic of anthrax killed entire herds of cattle and sheep in France in 1881. Pasteur used Koch's methods to isolate and grow the anthrax bacteria Koch had identified. Then Pasteur started some experiments to develop a vaccine that would make animals immune to the disease, just as Jenner had used cowpox fluid to make a vaccine for smallpox. But there was no natural mild form of anthrax, so Pasteur set out to "weaken" the anthrax bacteria. He found that by growing the bacteria at a higher temperature and for longer than usual (at 108°F [42°C] for eight to ten days), the bacteria would weaken. When the weakened bacteria were injected into animals, the animals did not get anthrax. They also developed immunity to the disease.

When swine fever was killing thousands of pigs in France, and more than a million pigs in the United States, Pasteur made a vaccine with weakened bacteria against the disease. He also developed a vaccine against rabies, although he never saw or isolated the organism that caused it. Like smallpox, rabies is caused by a virus, but whether Pasteur was working with an unseen virus or a visible bacterium, he proved that a weakened disease organism can be used to combat the disease itself. And that discovery opened the door to conquering many diseases.

3

KILLING
THE BEASTIES

Imagine having an operation without an anesthetic to kill the pain. Such agony would be unthinkable now, but even after anesthetics were discovered in the late 1800s, horrors after surgery continued. It was not unusual for an operation to be a success, only to have the patient die later from massive infections.

Joseph Lister, a professor of surgery in Edinburgh, Scotland, had read about Koch's discovery and Pasteur's theory that germs or disease microbes were in the air, in soil, and on all surfaces. Having seen uncontrollable infections after surgery, no matter how carefully he operated, Lister was convinced that the infections must be caused by germs outside the patients' bodies. So he decided to search for a way to combat these infections.

One day in 1865, Lister tried his new antiseptic method for the first time. Before he operated on a patient with a compound fracture of the leg, Lister scrubbed his hands and the patient's leg with carbolic acid, soaked the bandages and instruments in the acid, and had the acid sprayed in the air all during the operation. The acid worked. The patient did not develop any infections. It is hard to imagine now, but many

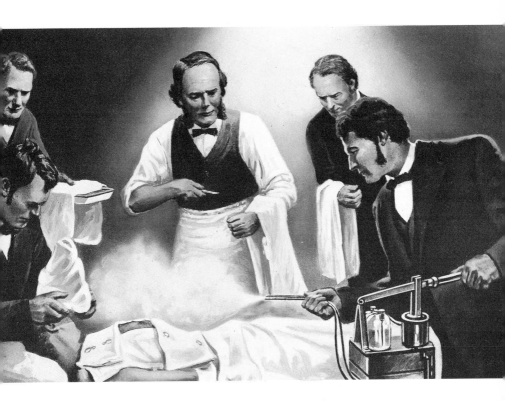

Joseph Lister directing his assistants in the use of carbolic acid spray during one of his antiseptic surgical operations. The carbolic acid kept bacteria from entering the patient's wounds and causing infections.

doctors opposed Lister's method at first. It was not until 1900 that antiseptic surgery became an accepted practice.

Although antiseptic techniques in hospitals will kill bacteria before they get into the body, we cannot live under antiseptic conditions. We breathe in bacteria, and we take them in with food and water. Even a scratch on the skin will let in bacteria. Yet we don't usually get a disease or an infection because the body has its own superb systems of defense.

Our main protective barrier against bacteria is the skin, which is made up of closely interlocking cells. Inside the skin, sweat and oil glands secrete acids that kill or prevent the growth of many bacteria. There is also a huge population of harmless bacteria living on the skin, and they protect their own territories from foreign bacteria that just might cause trouble.

All body openings are protected, too. The nose, mouth, throat, and windpipe are covered with fragile membranes and a layer of sticky mucus that can kill bacteria. Any bacteria that get past this mucus barrier are swept out of the windpipe by tiny hairs called cilia and into the throat, where they are swallowed. Bacteria that are swallowed face certain death by the acids in the stomach. Saliva and tears also contain anti-septic substances that protect the mouth and eyes.

Out of the billions of bacteria we are in contact with daily, some manage to get through the first defenses. Bacteria that enter through a cut in the skin are met by an inflammatory response. Some of the body's injured cells release histamine, a chemical that causes blood vessels near the wound to swell and bring more blood to the injury. When that spot becomes hot and red, we say it's inflamed. Chemicals in the blood quickly form a clot that seals off the cut and prevents more bacteria from getting in. The injured cells also release chemicals that attract bacteria-eating white cells called phagocytes. The phagocytes move through the injured area engulfing bacteria as though they were starving. As the battle goes on, the phagocytes fill up with dead and live bacteria. The phagocytes then die and form pus. Pus is simply the wreckage left from this war against infection.

Any bacteria that escape the phagocytes and are carried through the body, or that get into the body through the nose or mouth, are met by a third line of defense, the immune system. The fighters in this remarkable system are white cells called lymphocytes. At any given time, about two trillion lymphocytes are patrolling the blood and lymph systems, or are on duty in the spleen, tonsils, and lymph nodes. It is the job of the lymphocytes to detect all invaders—bacteria, fungi, viruses, and any other foreigners, including transplanted organs.

The moment bacteria are discovered, the lymphocytes divide and start churning out antibodies to kill or neutralize the invaders. Antibodies are chemicals that destroy specific invaders. For example, antibodies sent out against pneumonia bacteria fight only pneumonia bacteria; they do not stop tuberculosis bacteria. Different antibodies are made for each new invader, and it takes five to seven days to get production up to the maximum. Within the body, a race between the

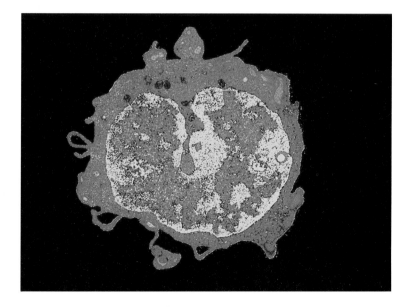

A human T-lymphocyte. Some T-lymphocytes control the body's immune system response to invaders. Others actually kill certain types of invading or infected cells.

25

reproducing bacteria and the immune system producing antibodies takes place. Sometimes, if the bacteria win, the person dies.

Lymphocytes also make memory cells that patrol the body, ready for instant battle if they recognize an old enemy. When an invader returns, the memory cells can start maximum production of antibodies immediately. Such a speedy response usually defeats the invader before there are any signs of a disease. Some memory cells last a lifetime, and they give immunity from disease for a lifetime. For example, once you have chicken pox, the memory cells keep you immune, and you will never get chicken pox again. A vaccine prevents a disease because it tricks the body's immune system into making memory cells against the disease without the person actually having had the disease.

Scientists haven't made vaccines to fight all infections because there are just too many invaders. A bacterium called a spirochete, for example, causes syphilis, a disease that is spread by sexual contact and from an infected mother to her unborn child. For centuries this devastating disease was feared because there was no way to stop it. Then in 1905, a German scientist, Paul Ehrlich, went to work on finding a cure for syphilis. He infected rabbits with the spirochete and began testing different arsenic compounds. In 1910, when he came to compound number 606, it killed the spirochete. After several hundred people had been treated successfully with 606, Ehrlich named the new drug Salvarsan, which means "saved by arsenic." Ehrlich called Salvarsan his "magic bullet" because it went directly to the disease organism and killed it without hurting any other cells in the body.

After Ehrlich's discovery, laboratories around the world began searching for magic bullets. They met with little success until 1935, when scientists at a German lab found the next major bacteria-killing drug. It was sulfanilamide, a drug

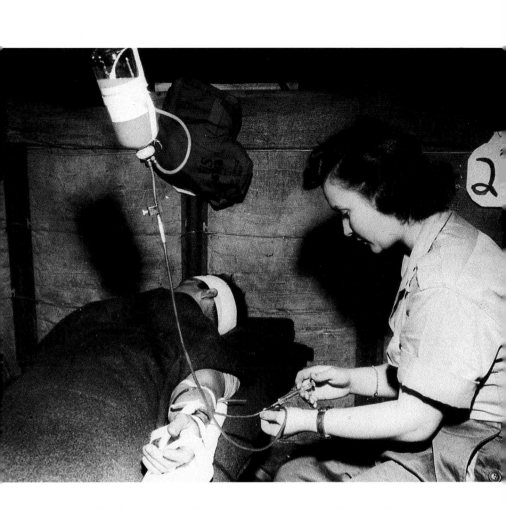

A sulfa drug being administered to a soldier. Since sulfa drugs first came into use, over 150 more effective versions have been developed. These drugs are still used today to treat some infections and are sometimes combined with other drugs.

that could stop general bacterial infections. Before sulfanilamide was discovered, people feared even simple scratches and pinpricks because the injuries could develop an infection that would rage through the body as blood poisoning. In 1936, Franklin Roosevelt, Jr., the son of the president of the

United States, was dying of blood poisoning. The president's wife, Eleanor, heard about the new sulfa drug and asked the German lab for help. Even though the United States and Germany were on the verge of war, the Germans airmailed the drug to Mrs. Roosevelt. It stopped the infection and saved the boy's life. During World War II, packets of sulfa were part of every first-aid kit, and the drug saved thousands of lives from bacterial infections picked up on the battlefields.

Penicillin turned out to be better than a magic bullet. It was a real wonder drug. One day in 1928, Alexander Fleming was cleaning up his lab at St. Mary's Hospital in London. He was checking a stack of petri dishes when he noticed some yellow mold growing over a culture of *Staphylococcus* bacteria in one of the dishes. The bacteria had been taken from boils on a patient in the hospital. All around the mold was a clear area where something from the mold had killed the bacteria. When Fleming spread the mold on petri dishes containing several different kinds of bacteria, he found that juice from the mold killed all the bacteria. Fleming named this bacteria-killing substance penicillin, after the name of the mold, *Penicillium notatum*. Even though Fleming didn't isolate penicillin's active chemical to make it into a usable drug, without his discovery there would have been no starting point for others.

Eleven years later in Britain, Howard Florey, an Australian, and Ernst Chain, a refugee from Germany, took up the project of producing penicillin. They isolated and purified the active chemical in the mold, but they couldn't persuade British drug companies to produce the penicillin. World War II was going badly for Britain at that time, and drug companies were working to capacity making drugs for the soldiers. So Florey and Chain secretly took the mold to the United States and asked for help. They eventually convinced four companies to work together to mass-produce

Alexander Fleming with a petri dish on which a colony of penicillin is growing. Inset: A penicillin colony (at the top) destroying the bacteria closest to it.

penicillin. Such cooperation among commercial drug makers and the government had never happened before, but everyone concerned knew what a difference such a drug could make in wartime. By 1943, enough penicillin was available to the Allied Armed Forces to save millions of lives, and a year later anyone could get the new wonder drug. Today, penicillin is no longer made from mold, but from chemicals that achieve the same results.

Knowing that soil is literally crawling with bacteria, molds, and other microbes, scientists began testing soil samples from all parts of the world in their search for the next wonder drug. One drug company sent envelopes to all its stockholders with instructions to mail back samples of soil from their backyards and gardens. Other companies asked for mold samples from missionaries, foreign correspondents, airline pilots, deep-sea divers, and anyone who traveled around the world. It was a great idea and it worked. Chloromycetin was found in a fungus from Venezuela. Aureomycin was made from an unknown fungus found in a sample of dirt from a backyard in Columbia, Missouri. Streptomycin came from a new mold found in the throat of a chicken in New Jersey. Terramycin was taken from a mold in Terre Haute, Indiana. In all, more than 5,000 different bacteria-killing drugs, called antibiotics, were discovered in the years following the penicillin breakthrough. Only 17 of those drugs became commercially successful, but that was enough to change the world of medicine forever. And scientists today are still looking for microbes that might be used to help save lives.

4
DIGEST, DECAY, AND DESTROY

The ultimate invader is one that gets inside another organism and stays there. Often the invader harms the organism, but sometimes this close relationship is beneficial. A cow grazing in a meadow is eating grass it can't digest, at least not until millions of bacteria and other microbes work on it. Like all plants, grass contains cellulose, a tough, protective, structural substance that forms plant cell walls. No animal can digest it. A cow's stomach, however, has four chambers, and two of these chambers contain large numbers of bacteria and other microbes that break down the tough cellulose in grass. They change the grass into glucose, which the cow's cells can use. Many extra vitamins and proteins are also added to a cow's diet from bacteria that are digested along with the grass, but these useful bacteria reproduce so fast that the dead ones are replaced in less than a day.

Wood is almost 100 percent cellulose, yet termites live on it. They eat it, but they must rely on bacteria in their gut to digest the cellulose. Boat owners hate shipworms, which are tiny, wormlike creatures that live in the ocean and spend their lives boring holes in wooden boat hulls, docks, and piers. Shipworms, too, need bacterial partners, which live in small glands connected to their intestines, to digest the cellulose in wood.

Like cows and termites, humans can't digest cellulose. We call the cellulose roughage, and it helps move waste materials out of our intestines. We, too, have bacteria in our intestines, but our bacteria, *E. coli*, have a different job. They eat undigested material, including cellulose. And in exchange for a warm, moist, protected habitat and all the food they can eat, the bacteria help keep our intestines in good condition. They also make vitamin K, which we need to help our blood clot. People who take antibiotics over long periods of time to fight infections often get diarrhea and intestinal upsets because antibiotics can't tell "good" bacteria from "bad." Antibiotics kill good *E. coli* bacteria along with bad infectious bacteria.

Even though scientists have known for a long time that bacteria live everywhere, they were surprised by what a team of scientists found in 1977. The team was exploring the floor of the Pacific Ocean in the U.S. Navy's three-person submarine, *Alvin*. Cruising near the Galagapos Islands at a depth of 8,000 feet (2,400 meters), they discovered underwater vents, like volcanoes, spewing out superheated water filled with hydrogen sulfide and carbon dioxide gases. They were amazed to see clams, tube worms, crabs, and "vent" fish living in the inky darkness around the vents. How could these animals grow and flourish in such a desolate environment? Where did they find food?

After the scientists in *Alvin* collected some of the animals and returned to their home base laboratories, they discovered sulfur bacteria living in the cells and tissue of the animals. Like green plants, these sulfur bacteria were able to combine water and carbon dioxide to make their own food. But plants need light as a source of energy to make food. In the black ocean depths, there is no light. Where did the sulfur bacteria find energy? It turned out the hydrogen sulfide gas provided the energy the sulfur bacteria needed to make food. And they made food for the animals in whose cells they lived as well as for themselves.

Bacteria don't live in our cells and make food for us, but they are absolutely essential to our lives and all other life on earth. If all microbes were suddenly wiped out, life on earth would be doomed. Nothing would rot. Without bacteria to decompose organic materials, every plant and animal would remain just where it died. It wouldn't be long before we would be knee-deep in dead organisms. Even if we buried all dead things, life on earth would gradually sputter out because the materials needed to make new living things would be locked up in the dead plants and animals.

If you take a walk in the woods you will see fungi of many kinds growing on dead trees and shrubs. Fungi are one of the first invaders to start the process of decay, and they make way for the next ones—the billions of microscopic bacteria that turn dead wood into rich forest soil.

Recycling is nothing new. Nature has been doing it for billions of years. By feeding on wastes and dead organisms, microbes break down the organisms into basic elements and return those materials to the soil where they can be used over again to make new living things. All organisms only borrow their atoms. During its lifetime, an organism continually rotates many of the chemicals it is made up of as nutrients are taken in and waste products are released. The fertilizers people put on lawns, gardens, and farm fields are nothing more than mixtures of chemical compounds of nitrogen, phosphorus, potassium, and sulfur. These are the same elements that are released directly into the soil by the action of the decomposers, the bacteria and other microbes that naturally maintain the fertility of soil.

Plants must have nitrogen in order to make their pro-

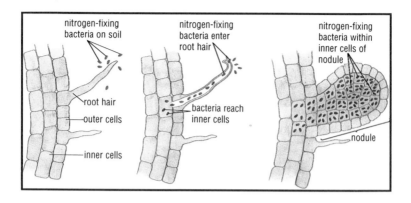

Nitrogen-fixing bacteria entering the root of a plant. The bacteria digest their way into a root hair and the plant's cells. The bacteria and cells multiply, forming a nodule. The bacteria then provide nitrates directly to the plant.

teins. Even though the air is 78 percent nitrogen gas, plants can't use the gas without the help of nitrogen-fixing bacteria. These bacteria take nitrogen gas from the air and change it into nitrates, which plants can use. As long ago as 300 B.C., Greek farmers knew that if they planted clover or peas in poor soil, other crops planted in that same soil the following year would grow very well. What they didn't know was that nitrogen-fixing bacteria lived in the tiny nodules, or bumps, on the roots of plants like clover, peas, beans, and soybeans. In their partnerships with bacteria, these plants provide food for the bacteria, and the bacteria provide nitrates so the plants can make proteins. Peas and beans are good sources of protein because of these bacteria.

The volcanic island of Krakatau, in Indonesia, was once covered by lush tropical forests. It was teeming with animals. But in 1883, the volcano erupted in an explosion so violent that all life on the island was wiped out. Nothing survived. But in a few years, a dark green mat began to grow on the ash

The Krakatau volcano. The explosion in 1883, which killed off all living things on the island, was one of the largest volcanic eruptions in modern times.

that had buried the island. After a while, the green mat became thick enough to support plants that sprouted from seeds that drifted in or were dropped by birds. The green mat was a huge colony of bacteria, the kind that used to be called blue-green algae, but are now called cyanobacteria.

Cyanobacteria are some of the world's most independent organisms. They make their own food by photo- synthesis, just like plants do, but some of them can also act like nitrogen-fixing bacteria to fertilize themselves. In Asia, rice has been grown in the same fields for centuries without adding fertilizer because cyanobacteria live there and fertilize the ground.

Decay bacteria work for us by providing fertile soil, but they also work against us by spoiling food. Microbes can change the taste, odor, and consistency of foods, and sometimes they can turn food into something lethal. Airborne bacteria may float into food on dust particles. Bacteria may be hurled into food by coughs and sneezes, and they may drop into it from clothes and hair. Bacteria on a cook's hands, and on knives, spoons, and pots, may also be added to food. Fortunately, most of these bacteria are harmless, and fresh meat and vegetable tissues are not an easy meal for bacteria because the cells are intact. Cooking the food kills almost all bacteria, except for a few spores that survive. But cooking also breaks down the meat and vegetable cells, making them open to attack by bacteria. As food cools, it becomes a perfect culture medium for bacterial growth, and more microbes from the air may be added when food is served.

The longer food left at the end of a meal sits out at room temperature, the more bacteria get into it, and the more dangerous the food becomes. Some bacteria change meat and vegetable proteins into ptomaines, a deadly group of toxic chemicals. Other bacteria secrete their own toxic substances. Food poisoning can range from a minor upset stomach to one severe enough for the person to need hospital care. Refrigeration does not kill bacteria or destroy toxins, but it does stop bacteria from reproducing. Small numbers of bacteria can be destroyed by our immune system, but large numbers can overpower the system and cause sickness.

Food can be protected from bacteria and other microbes in many ways. Drying and salting are probably the oldest methods of protecting and preserving food. Although cave dwellers knew nothing about bacteria, they found they could keep dried meat for long periods of time and not get sick after eating it. And even though some bacteria grow in oceans and the Great Salt Lake, they cannot live in very high concentrations of salt.

Today, people may protect and preserve food by canning it in glass jars that have been boiled to kill bacteria. Most of the canning done in factories uses superheated steam, which sterilizes the cans and the food, killing both bacteria and their spores. Freezing and freeze-drying kill many bacteria and stop the growth of those that do survive. Chemical preservatives may be added to food to keep it fresh. Preservatives usually don't kill microbes, but they do stop microbes from growing and reproducing. Food may also be protected from microbes by pickling it in vinegar, which is too acid for most microbes to live in. And few bacteria can survive in jams, jellies, and syrups because of their strong sugar solutions.

Irradiation is a new process being used to help make food safe. In 1990, after many years of testing, the Food and

Two ways of preserving food. The fish are being dried by the traditional Inuit (Eskimo) method. The grapefruit are being placed in position for an irradiation experiment.

Drug Administration (FDA) announced that irradiation was a safe and effective way to control bacterial food poisoning in chickens and turkeys. The process uses radiation to damage the genetic material in bacteria so the organisms cannot survive or reproduce in food. Irradiation is now being used in more than 35 countries and is endorsed by the World Health Organization. People in the United States, however, have been slow to accept this process because of safety concerns. After reviewing all the experiments, the FDA maintains that irradiation is safe. The FDA says that "irradiation does not make food radioactive and therefore does not increase human exposure to radiation."

With their unusual appetites, bacteria can make a feast out of some of the most inedible things you can imagine. Roads paved with asphalt deteriorate, especially in warm, moist climates, but it can't always be blamed on poor construction. The deterioration may be the fault of bacteria with an appetite for petroleum and products made from petroleum, like asphalt. These bacteria can ruin cars, too. If the bacteria multiply in large oil and gasoline storage tanks, they produce sulfur or sulfur dioxide, which contaminates the oil or gas. When used as fuel in cars, the contaminated oil or gas corrodes engine parts.

Sulfur bacteria can destroy iron. Wherever it is exposed to water and oxygen, iron rusts. Iron pipes buried deep in the ground get wet, but they are not exposed to oxygen. Yet these pipes sometimes corrode faster than iron pipes on the surface. Sulfur bacteria are to blame. With the help of water and natural sulfates in the soil, sulfur bacteria attack gas, water, and drainage pipes made from iron. The bacteria need very little sulfate, and they are in no hurry. The fastest corrosion of a water main took about three years. In 1990, in the United States, bacteria caused billions of dollars worth of damage to underground iron pipes, which is one reason why

38

Rusted water pipe. Water in supply pipes that have been rusted and contaminated by sulfur bacteria are a health hazard.

plastic pipes are being used to replace the old iron ones. Plastic is safe from microbes—so far. But since the world began, bacteria have changed and adapted to all kinds of new conditions and substances. Will some develop that live on plastic?

Concrete is also a hearty meal for microbes. Most city sewer pipes are made from concrete. Every once in a while when the top section of a sewer collapses, shutting down the system, it is another example of sulfur bacteria at work. As microbes go about their business of decomposing human sewage, hydrogen sulfide gas is given off. The gas rises to the tops of the sewer pipes. Waiting at the tops of the pipes are sulfur bacteria that change the hydrogen sulfide gas into sulfuric acid, which slowly destroys the tops of the concrete pipes. Buildings and statues made from stone that contains even small amounts of sulfur compounds can meet the same fate as sewer pipes. Some ancient temples in Indochina that were built on sulfur-rich soil have been almost completely destroyed, and statues in Paris and other cities have been badly damaged by sulfur microbes.

Oil spills and toxic chemical spills cause terrible water pollution, but any slow-moving body of water can be turned into a smelly, toxic mess by microbes. This microbe pollution can be just as damaging and difficult to stop as a toxic spill. When plant life dies in water, bacteria decompose it and turn its nutrients loose in the water for new plants to use. As more plants grow and die, decay bacteria, which use up oxygen, multiply. This cycle snowballs until the oxygen-loving decay bacteria use up most of the oxygen in the water. A fast-running stream is constantly renewing its oxygen, but a slow-moving body of water can't get enough oxygen to keep ahead of the microbes. As the oxygen supply decreases, fish and other animals die, adding more organic material for decay. Finally, when the oxygen in the water is low enough, the sulfur bacteria take over. You can tell they are there because the stagnant water smells like rotten eggs—the smell of hydrogen sulfide. The hydrogen sulfide is toxic. It kills whatever life remains in the water. What is left is a black, oily-looking, smelly, lifeless patch of pollution.

These and many other microbes continually decay, destroy, and pollute our natural and human-made environment. But we've learned that some of these same microbes can be put to work in other ways. They can be adapted, changed, and used to benefit ourselves and our environment.

5
PUTTING
BACTERIA
TO WORK

The same bacteria and other microbes that turn a body of water into a stinking mess can also make our lives and environment clean and comfortable. In the Middle Ages, before sewage treatment, living in a city was like living in a pigsty. People used alleys for bathrooms. They dumped chamber pots and garbage into the streets. And they almost never took baths. Even men wore heavy perfumes to hide the odors. One summer in London, Parliament did not meet because the stench from the Thames River was too sickening. Rivers and streams became open sewers, and epidemics of cholera and typhoid were common.

Today's sewage treatment plants depend on both oxygen-loving and oxygen-hating bacteria. In Baltimore, Maryland, four million pounds (1.8 million kilograms) of bacteria feed on sewage in a new treatment plant. First, heavy solids, called sludge, are separated from small particles dissolved and suspended in the liquid sewage. Then the liquid is sprayed on a bed of stones covered by a film of bacteria and fungi that decompose the organic wastes. The sludge is mixed with air and stirred in a settling tank where oxygen-loving bacteria begin to digest it. The sludge is then pumped into large, heated tanks, where oxygen-hating bacteria break it down into sludge gas, which is mainly methane. This sludge gas, also called biogas, runs the machinery at the sewage plant and heats the tanks. In India and China, families and communities use biogas to generate electricity and heat. India is also experimenting with ways to use cow dung, straw, and other agricultural wastes for energy.

In 1989, the *Exxon Valdez* tanker spilled 11 million gallons (41.6 million liters) of oil off the coast of Alaska. The slick covered more than 100 square miles (260 square kilometers), harming thousands of fish, birds, and sea mammals and spoiling beaches. When an offshore oil well in the Gulf of Mexico blew out in 1979, more than 100 million gallons (378.5 million liters) of oil were released. Some of this oil washed up on beaches in Texas, 600 miles (966 kilometers) away. And an even greater amount of oil was spilled in the Persian Gulf during Desert Storm in 1991.

Cleaning up all this spilled oil is a monumental task, but scientists have found that the same bacteria that eat asphalt and destroy roads can also eat and destroy oil. Sawdust sprinkled over a spill absorbs oil and sinks to the bottom of the water, where the oil-eating bacteria slowly decompose the oil. Powdered white clay also absorbs oil, but instead of sinking, it floats like small, edible islands on which the bacteria feed. In one experiment with this clay, almost three-quarters of a test spill was eaten by bacteria in just five weeks, a job that would take nature 55 years. One researcher said, "You get these floating dinner plates of oil, and the bacteria just love 'em."

The first genetically designed, oil-gobbling bacteria were made in 1972. Since then, other labs have been breeding better and better oil-eating bacteria. And researchers are constantly on the watch for a super oil-eater that could be

An oil cleanup experiment using bacteria that eat petroleum products. Oil is poured into a test tank. Then powdered white clay is sprinkled on the oil, forming "islands" that the bacteria attack. The small amount of oil remaining will eventually be eaten by the bacteria.

raised in batches large enough to be spread by airplane on an oil slick.

Coast to coast, the steel tanks in thousands of old gas stations are corroding and leaking gasoline into the soil. This gasoline seeps into the groundwater and releases toxic, cancer-causing substances like benzene. Once again, microbes have come to the rescue. By adding phosphorus and nitrogen to the soil and pumping in air, researchers have found they can increase the number of microbes that naturally feed on these toxic substances. It has been a slow process, but the gas-contaminated soil is being cleaned up.

What can a community do when abandoned refineries and other industries leave the soil full of toxic compounds? One common solution was to dig up the soil and truck it to landfills in another state, which just pushed the problem onto another community. But now there are about 50 bioremediation companies that use microbes to clean up contaminated sites. And bioremediation costs about one-third as much as digging up the soil and trucking it away.

Gold is separated from its ore in a process that uses the poison cyanide. After separation, the cyanide is usually flushed into a local stream along with other dissolved minerals from the ore. The Homestake Mine in South Dakota, which is the largest gold mine in North America, had been flushing cyanide into Whitewood Creek for 100 years. Finally the creek became so polluted it was sterile. Nothing could live in it. However, when the creek water was tested, scientists found some bacteria that were not only resistant to cyanide, but that actually ate the poison for food. They raised these bacteria in great numbers and put them in a series of tanks. Now the contaminated wastewater from the mine first flows slowly through the tanks, where the bacteria gobble up the cyanide. Then the water goes back into the creek. The creek is now clean again and thriving with life.

Scientists in laboratories around the world are always looking for new ways to use microbes with useful appetites. In an old landfill, researchers found two bacteria and a fungus that can remove paint. Once the paint is removed, another bacterium, one that was found in a junk pile, eats the old paint. At the University of West Florida, researchers studied more than 20,000 mutants of a single strain of bacteria to find one that breaks down TCE (trichloroethylene), a toxin found in many industrial solvents. Another harmful substance, creosote, is a corroding, burning chemical, but it is a great wood preservative that keeps railroad ties and telephone poles from rotting. It was almost impossible to clean up the soil around abandoned railroads and other sites until the right bacteria were found to destroy the creosote.

Dioxins, DDT, and PCBs are tough, stable chemicals that withstand attacks by most microbes. These highly toxic chemicals can pollute water and soil for long periods of time, causing death and illness in animals and humans. Scientists have found bacteria that slowly destroy these chemicals, but they are also attempting to breed and encourage the growth of more active bacteria that would work more quickly.

Microbes go to work every day. They make vitamins that are used as food additives and for making vitamin supplements. Vitamin C is made by bacteria growing on a plant product called sorbitol, and riboflavin, one of the B vitamins, is made from yeast. Enzymes made by other bacteria are used to separate flax fibers for linen and to remove hair from cowhides before they are tanned into leather. Similar bacterial enzymes are put into laundry detergents to dissolve stains.

Scientists are presently experimenting with a bacterium that produces tiny fibers called macrofibers. These fibers are strong, flexible, porous, and biodegradable. They may be used to make better ceramic products, electronics equipment, and so-called intelligent materials that can adapt to their changing environment.

Chemical pesticides used on crops soak into the ground and kill beneficial insects and microbes. These chemicals also form a toxic film on fruits and vegetables that is considered dangerous for humans to eat. Much better than chemical control of pests is biological control, such as the action of a bacterium called Bacillus thuringiensis, or Bt. Bt contains a protein that eats through the gut of a caterpillar. When sprayed or dusted on crops, the bacteria kill the caterpillars

45

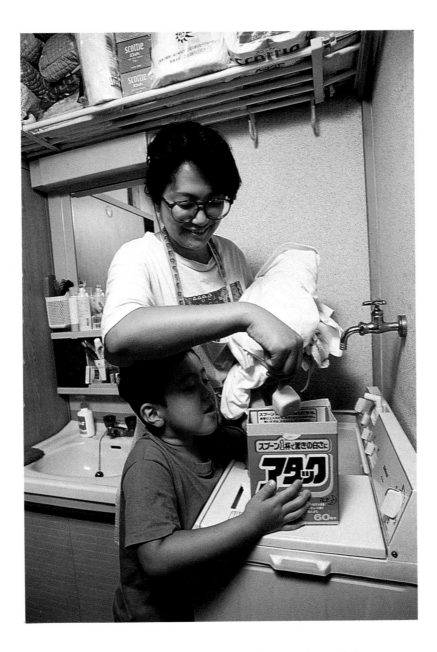

A Japanese detergent, called Attack, that uses bacterial enzymes for better cleaning and to digest stains. The bacteria that produce the enzymes were found in a rice field.

of gypsy moths, bagworms, and other insect pests that destroy the crops. Another kind of bacteria produce spores that kill insects. When the spores are spread on the ground, they are eaten by grubs, or larvae, of the Japanese beetle and other insects. The spores kill the grubs. The bacteria then use the dead grubs as food to produce more spores, which infect and kill more grubs.

Without microbes there would be no cheese. Nobody knows who made the first cheese, but ancient legends tell of a traveler who carried a water pouch made from the stomach of a goat or a sheep. One day he filled the pouch with milk. After he had trudged all day through the hot desert, he opened the pouch for a drink, but only a thin trickle of sour, white, watery liquid came out. He cut open the pouch to find it filled with a mass of soft curds that had a strange but pleasant taste. Bacteria left in the animal's stomach had separated the milk into watery whey and solid cheese curds. Today, the kind of bacterium or mold used to make a cheese determines the kind of cheese it will be. For example, cottage cheese is made by a bacterium, while blue-veined cheeses are made by molds.

Other bacteria turn milk into other foods. One kind turns pasteurized skim milk into buttermilk. A starter culture of another kind of bacteria is added to milk to make yogurt. People who make yogurt at home always save a few teaspoons of the yogurt because it contains enough live bacteria to use as a starter for another batch.

By the time coffee beans get to a store they have already been worked on by microbes. Coffee beans consist of two berries in a hard shell. Even after they are run through a pulping machine, bits of the shell still stick to the beans. So the beans are put into a tank where bacteria break down the remaining bits of shell and free the beans, which are then washed, dried, and roasted. And before cocoa beans can develop their chocolate flavor, they must be fermented by bacteria and yeast, then dried and heated.

Without microbes we would not have sauerkraut, pickles, or olives to eat. Despite its German name, sauerkraut was first made in China in the third century B.C. It is said that an

Captain James Cook and some of his crew. On his three-year exploration of the South Pacific, Cook prevented scurvy among his crew by having the sailors observe strict dietary rules.

emperor tried to preserve cabbage by shredding it and putting it in a bowl of rice wine. Bacteria on the cabbage grew in the wine and fermented the cabbage into a new food. This food turned out to be very nutritious and especially high in vitamin C. Lack of vitamin C causes scurvy, a disease that was once common among sailors. With no way to keep vitamin C-rich fruit fresh on long voyages, the sailors didn't get any vitamin C and developed scurvy. In 1772, when Captain James Cook made his famous voyages in the South Pacific, not one of the sailors in his crew got scurvy because they ate 30,000 pounds (13,600 kilograms) of vitamin C-rich sauerkraut.

Silage is food made for cattle from chopped corn, grasses, and legumes. This food material is stored in silos, or trenches, where the sauerkraut bacteria ferment it. The material is packed so tightly in the silos that all air is squeezed out. But an oxygen-free environment is where the oxygen-hating bacteria thrive. During fermentation, the bacteria produce lactic acid as a waste product, but it's not wasted. Lactic acid stops the growth of bacteria that would decay and spoil the silage, or sauerkraut for that matter.

6

TINKERING WITH BACTERIA

Scientists probably know more about the workings of *E. coli* bacteria than about any other single cell. Experiments on *E. coli* cells have helped researchers understand how human cells work, and they have also created new jobs for the bacteria.

Most cells have a nucleus. The nucleus holds all the cell's genetic information in structures called chromosomes. The chromosomes are composed of DNA, which carries the genetic information in the form of a code. Each sequence of codes in a DNA molecule that determines a specific trait or characteristic is called a gene.

A bacterial cell does not have a nucleus. Its single chromosome is just a double strand of DNA, folded several thousand times, floating loose in the cell. But a bacterium also contains several tiny rings of DNA called plasmids. The plasmids contain only a few genes. None of these genes is essential to the life of the bacterium, but they do give it certain advantages. Plasmid genes determine the cell's resistance to chemicals, the kinds of materials the cell can break down and use for food, and the special enzymes it can make. One type of plasmid, which scientists call the R plasmid, carries genes that give the bacterium resistance to antibiotics. Plasmids are

Plasmids from E. coli *bacteria. Plasmids are used in recombinant DNA research to transfer genes from one cell to another.*

also known to pick up genes from other plasmids or from bacterial chromosomes and carry them to a new cell.

Plasmids move in and out of bacteria easily, which is why scientists have been able to tinker with them using a technique called genetic engineering. A plasmid can be taken out of a bacterial cell and snipped open with special enzymes that work like biological scissors. These enzymes are so precise they can open a strand of DNA at a specific location. A new gene can then be inserted and "glued" in place with another enzyme. When the recombined plasmids, with their new DNA, are put in a solution of calcium chloride with normal *E. coli* bacteria and heated, the new plasmids enter the bacteria and become part of the genetic code of the *E. coli*. From then on, every time the *E. coli* bacteria divide, the foreign gene that has been added to the plasmids is duplicated, too. In each case, a new organism is created, one with a new genetic code.

Some people are opposed to the recombining, or joining, of pieces of DNA from two different species. They are concerned that this recombinant DNA is not safe. Could a new gene make bacteria that are harmful to people or plants or animals? What might happen if experimental *E. coli* bacteria escaped from a laboratory?

The National Institutes of Health has a list of research rules and conditions for scientists to follow. The rules specify certain experiments that should not be done at all. No one, for example, is allowed to recombine genes from a high-risk, disease-causing organism. The rules for laboratory procedures cover a wide range of safeguards, from the use of sterile conditions to isolation in a sealed laboratory where researchers enter through air locks and change into special protective clothing. At the end of the day, workers must shower and leave their special clothing inside the lab. Any materials leaving the laboratory are either steam sterilized or

A technician operating a "gene gun." The gun injects new genetic material into the nucleus of a cell. The cell then produces more cells with the new genetic makeup.

passed through a disinfectant bath. Even the air is incinerated before it goes outside. And most important, scientists have designed a strain of *E. coli* bacteria for recombinant experiments that cannot survive outside the controlled conditions of a laboratory.

Recombined *E. coli* bacteria should probably be called the workhorses of medicine because so many of them provide new drugs and cures. Today, insulin is made faster, better, and cheaper than ever before by engineered *E. coli*. Four million people in the United States need insulin to treat diabetes, a disorder of the pancreas. Before genetic engineering, insulin was made from pancreases taken from pigs and cows that were slaughtered for food. Now, in sterilized tanks three stories high, trillions of *E. coli* bacteria make insulin. The advantage of this genetically engineered insulin is that the bacteria are making human insulin, which has none of the side effects that can occur with insulin taken from animals.

Every year, some babies are born who will never grow to a normal size because their bodies cannot produce enough growth hormone. Before recombinant DNA, a few children were treated with human growth hormone obtained from donated human pituitary glands. However, very small amounts of hormone could be extracted from each gland, and very few people donated the glands. But since a gene for the human growth hormone has been spliced into *E. coli,* the bacteria have been churning out ample amounts of growth hormone for all the children who need it.

Hemophilia is a disorder in which blood does not clot, and a cut or bruise can be fatal because a person could bleed to death. In most cases of hemophilia, the person can't make antihemophilic globulin, a substance necessary for blood clotting. But since the gene that makes the globulin was spliced into *E. coli*, it is mass-produced and readily available to anyone with hemophilia.

Result of an experiment with genetically engineered rat growth hormone. The mouse with a new gene for the growth hormone grew to nearly twice the size of the mouse without the new gene.

Genetic engineers have also been solving agricultural problems. A bacterial spray called Bt was developed to kill caterpillars that were destroying crops. It had one big drawback, though. The enzyme in the bacteria that eats through the caterpillar's gut is destroyed by sunlight, which means the spray had to be applied as often as once a week. But when scientists transferred the gene that makes this enzyme into another kind of bacteria, they solved the problem. They used *Pseudomonas* bacteria, which have a tough, two-layer outer wall that protects the enzyme from light. As a result, spray made from these recombined bacteria lasts much longer in the field.

Recombined DNA techniques work well on animal cells, but plants have cell walls that most bacteria can't get through.

Most of the bacteria that *can* penetrate plant cell walls are harmful. But scientists have found ways to work with some of them, especially Agrobacterium, which causes crown gall disease in plants. The scientists found the gene for this disease on a plasmid, removed it, and put in its place the Bt gene they wanted to transfer. The Agrobacteria became successful gene messengers, carrying the Bt enzyme into cotton plants. Now whole fields of cotton plants are making their own natural pesticide against caterpillars. Hopefully, other pesticide-type genes that can be spliced into plants will be found so we can reduce or eliminate the use of harmful chemical sprays and dusts.

In midwinter, tomatoes bought in stores in colder climates often taste like cardboard compared to vine-ripened tomatoes picked from a garden in summer or fall. In 1994, the

Cotton plant after an experiment with inserting the gene for Bt. The boll on the right was protected by the Bt gene. The two other bolls, which did not receive the Bt gene, show damage from pests that attack cotton plants.

FDA approved a new, good-tasting tomato with the trademark name Flavr Savr that is raised in a greenhouse and engineered to stay fresh for a long time. Researchers have also found a gene that prolongs the sweetness of peas and another gene that increases the starch in potatoes by 60 percent. The extra starch decreases the amount of cooking oil that soaks into the potatoes, solving the problem of greasy French fries and oily potato chips.

Some day we may not have to spread fertilizer on lawns, gardens, and farms because the plants will make their own. Scientists are looking for genes in the kind of bacteria that take nitrogen from the air and fix, or change, it into nitrates in the soil. If those genes can be spliced into plants, the plants themselves will be able to fix the nitrogen and fertilize themselves. If the genes cannot be found, it may be possible to find the genes in beans, peas, and other legumes that attract nitrogen-fixing bacteria to live in nodules on their roots. If those genes can be engineered into plants that live in nitrogen-poor soil, it will be possible to raise crops where none grow now. When these bacterial genes are spliced into plants, scientists will constantly be on guard against the possibility that the spliced genes might be harmful in the wrong organism.

An amazing anticancer drug called TAXOL, made from the bark of yew trees, was discovered in the early 1990s. But since so much bark is needed to make the drug, the demand for TAXOL soon became greater than the supply of bark. It was feared that yew trees would become extinct in a few years. But two researchers at Montana State University have discovered a fungus that can also be used to make TAXOL. If it turns out that drug companies can't easily mass-produce this fungus, they will probably try splicing the TAXOL-making gene from the fungus into the reliable old microbe factory, *E. coli*.

So far, the benefits of recombinant DNA seem to outweigh any possible problems. And although genetic engineering is a new technology for scientists, it has been used by bacteria for millions of years. Bacteria have exchanged plasmids containing genes that allow them to change enough to adapt to different environments. Only a few years after the widespread use of penicillin began, doctors found large numbers of bacteria had become resistant to the antibiotic drug. At the time penicillin was discovered there probably existed a few bacteria that had a natural resistance to it. As more penicillin was used to combat infectious bacterial diseases, the nonresistant bacteria were killed. But the remaining resistant bacteria were able to live and reproduce in this changed environment. These bacteria developed two different methods of resistance. In one method, the bacteria produce an enzyme that breaks down penicillin before it can bind with the enzymes that help the bacteria produce their cell walls. During the past 50 years, plasmids have passed the gene containing the code for this enzyme to most types of bacteria that attack the human body. In the other method, bacteria have changed their cell wall enzymes so penicillin cannot bind with them. Resistance has been found in almost every type of bacteria that has been fought with antibiotics, and some strains of bacteria are resistant to several different antibiotics. Antibiotics did not make the genes resistant, but they caused rapid spreading of the genes.

Ten years ago, doctors thought infectious bacterial diseases had been conquered. But in the United States today, thousands of surgery patients in hospitals are dying every year from infections caused by resistant bacteria. Several resistant strains of bacteria, causing diseases such as pneumonia, meningitis, and children's ear infections, are also spreading rapidly throughout the country. Tuberculosis is now the leading cause of death from infectious diseases worldwide, but it had been under control in the United States until 1985. Then the number of cases started to increase, and by 1991, one-third of all tuberculosis cases in New York City were found to be resistant to one or more antibiotics.

In 1990 a rare but deadly type of streptococcus killed Muppet creator Jim Henson. Another form of this bacterium made headlines in 1994 as the "flesh-eating bacteria." In one case, all the muscles in a man's arm were eaten away, and the damage was done in just two days. The bacteria are not yet resistant to penicillin, but the infection develops rapidly because the bacteria divide every 45 minutes. The Centers for Disease Control reported that the streptococcus infected 10,000 to 15,000 people in the United States in 1993, but it was almost nonexistent just five years earlier.

Laboratories around the world are searching for new antibiotics or trying to change old antibiotics to defeat new varieties and resistant bacteria's defenses. But most bacteria are harmless, and many could be helpful. Scientists are just beginning to find the microbes that might change the way we live. What other miraculous medicines might be made from bacteria? Which bacteria might help feed the world? Which bacteria might eat the increasing piles of garbage or clean up oil spills? Almost anything seems possible, so never underestimate the power of these tiny invaders.

GLOSSARY

agar: a jellylike substance used in making cultures for microorganisms.

anthrax: a contagious and often fatal disease usually found in sheep and cattle that may be caught by humans.

antibody: a protein produced by certain white blood cells that attacks foreign substances in the body.

asexual reproduction: the production of offspring from one parent.

bacterium: a microscopic one-celled organism that does not have a nucleus.

binary fission: a type of sexual reproduction in which one cell divides into two identical cells.

botulism: a deadly disease caused by a bacterium called botulin, which may be found in canned foods not properly heated.

chromosome: a tiny particle in the nucleus of a cell that carries the gene.

clone: an organism that is genetically identical to its parent.

conjugation: a type of asexual reproduction in simple organisms by which genetic material is exchanged.

culture medium: a fluid or solid containing nutrients for the artificial growing of organisms.

DDT: an insecticide that does not easily break down but is especially toxic to fish and birds.

dioxin: a group of chemical compounds that are some of the most toxic of all human-made substances.

DNA (Deoxyribonucleic acid): an acid found in the nucleus of a living cell; contains the codes needed to build proteins and carries the genetic information about an organism.

E. coli (Escherichia coli): a bacterium normally found in the large intestines of humans, where it makes vitamin K and helps maintain the health of the large intestine.

enzyme: a protein produced in living cells that controls chemical reactions within the body.

flagellum: a long, whiplike tail on some protozoans that allows them to move.

gene: the minute part of a chromosome that holds genetic information and determines a specific characteristic of an organism.

grub: a soft, thick, wormlike larva of an insect.

immunity: resistance to a disease or poison.

larva: the wormlike, young form of an insect that looks very different from the adult.

lymphocyte: a type of white blood cell that produces antibodies.

microbe: a germ, or microorganism.

microorganism: an organism too small to be seen except with a microscope.

mutant: a new variety of plant or animal carrying a gene or chromosome that has undergone mutation.

mutation: a change within a gene or chromosome resulting in a new characteristic that is inherited.

nitrogen-fixing: the process by which certain bacteria in the soil take nitrogen gas from the air and change it into nitrates, a compound useful to plants.

pasteurization: the process by which food is heated to a high enough temperature and for a long enough time to destroy harmful bacteria that can spoil the food.

PCBs: a group of industrial compounds that do not easily break down and are highly toxic, especially to wildlife.

phagocyte: a type of white blood cell that engulfs and destroys bacteria.

plasmid: a small circular molecule of DNA found in bacteria.

protozoan: a microscopic, one-celled animal.

pupa: the stage between the larva and adult of many insects; some are enclosed in a cocoon.

spirochete: a type of bacteria characterized by its very long, thin, spiral shape.

spontaneous generation: the false belief that living organisms could develop from nonliving materials.

spore: a single bacterial cell covered with a special protective coat that allows it to remain in a resting, or dormant, state.

vaccine: a substance made from dead or weakened bacteria or viruses used to inoculate a person in order to prevent a disease and produce an immunity to it; a vaccine works by causing the body to develop antibodies to the disease organisms.

FURTHER READING

Aaseng, Nathan. *The Disease Fighters*. Minneapolis: Lerner, 1987.

Anderson, Lucia. *The Smallest Life Around Us*. New York: Crown, 1978.

Asimov, Isaac. *How Did We Find Out About Germs?* New York: Walker, 1974.

Bender, Lionel. Around the Home. New York: Franklin Watts, 1991.

Canault, Nina. *Incredibly Small*. New York: New Discovery Books, 1993.

Lang, Susan S. *Invisible Bugs and Other Creepy Creatures That Live with You*. New York: Sterling, 1992.

Nardo, Don. *Germs: Mysterious Microorganisms*. San Diego: Lucent, 1991.

Sabin, Francine. *Microbes and Bacteria*. Mahwah, New Jersey: Troll, 1985.

INDEX